AMAZING COLORING BOOKS

For Kids Beautiful Animals

THIS BOOK BELONGS TO

TO

SHARK

KANGAROO

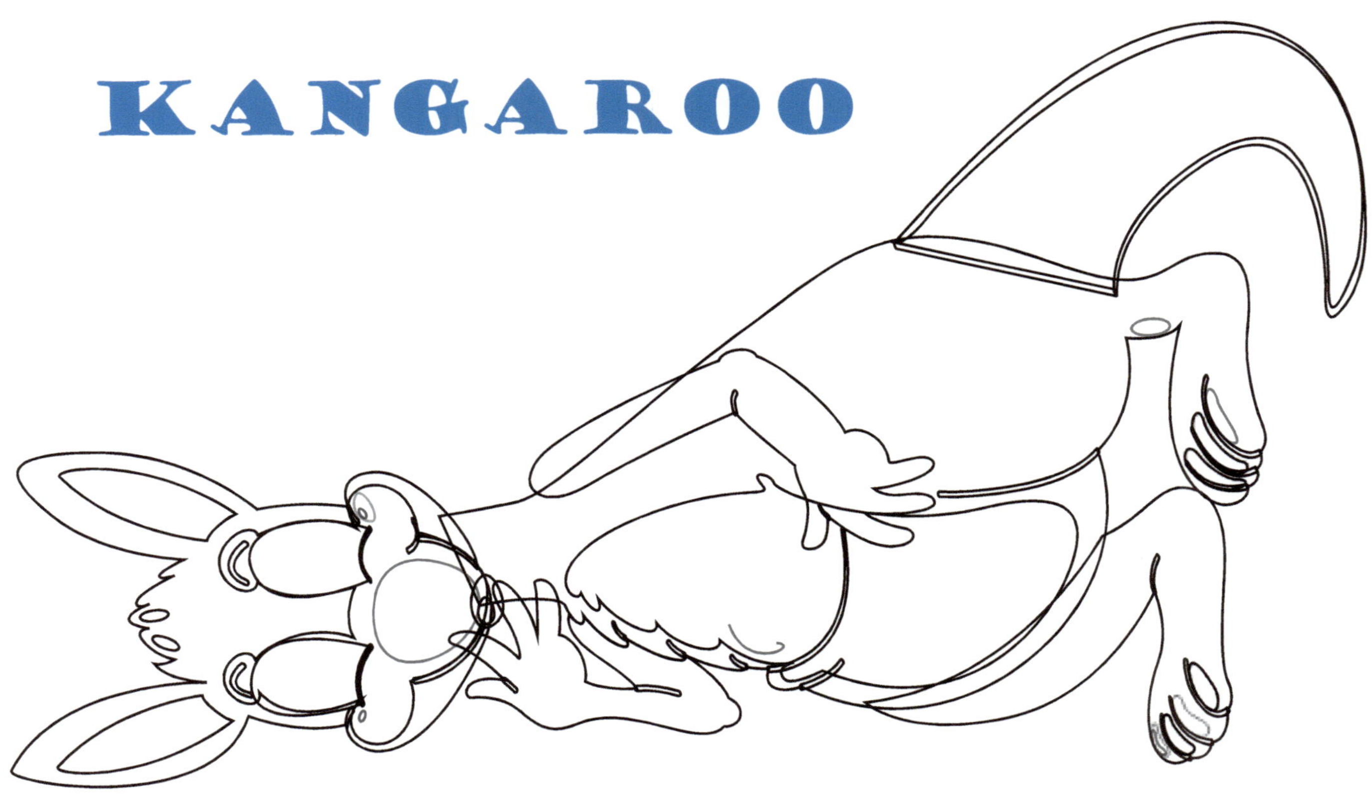

CROW

Draw you are a hero

HUNTER

Draw you are a hero

DRAWING THIS HORSE

HEN

RABBIT

FIND AND WRITE THE NAMES OF THE OTHER ANIMOTS

Draw you are a hero

Draw you are a hero

Draw you are a hero

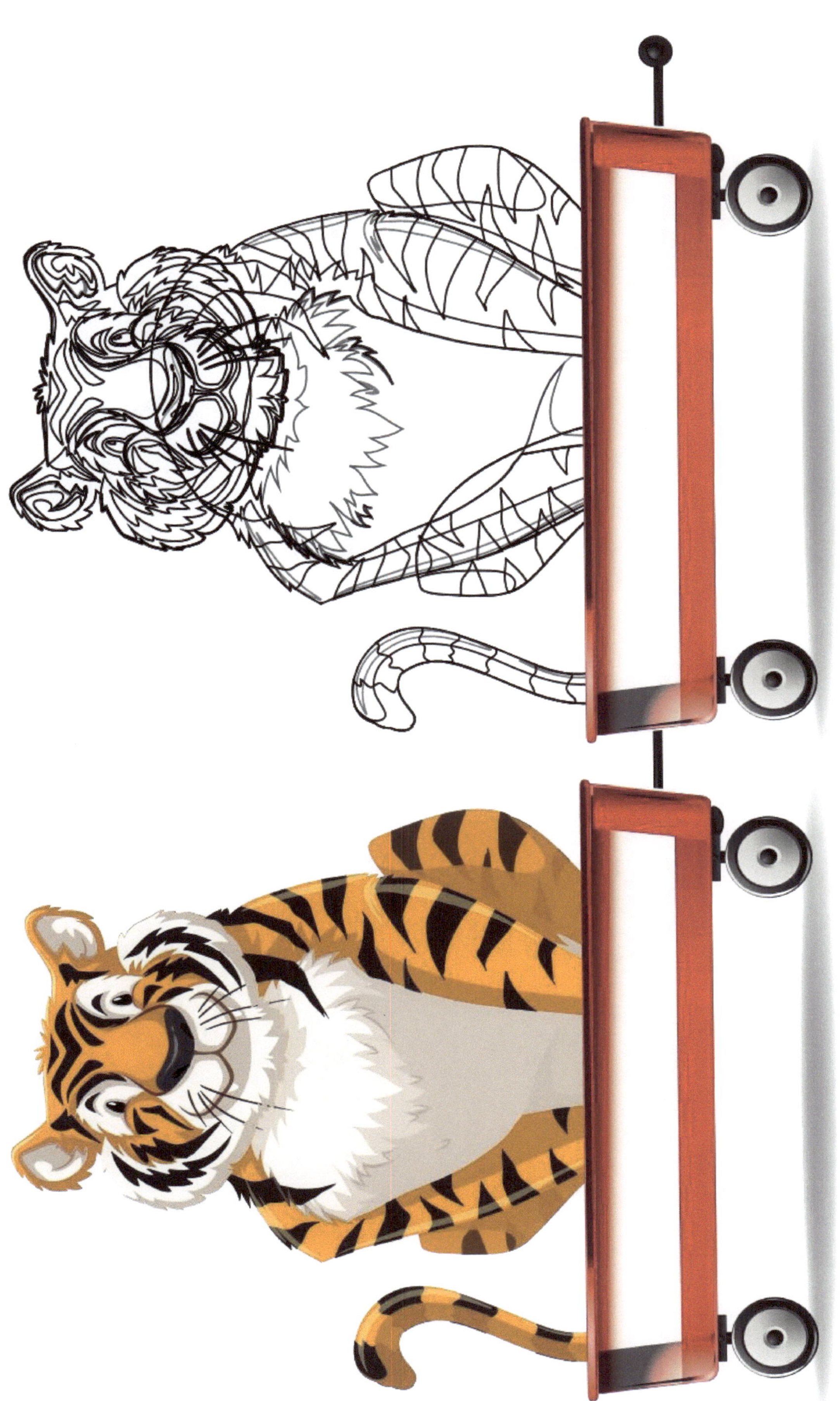

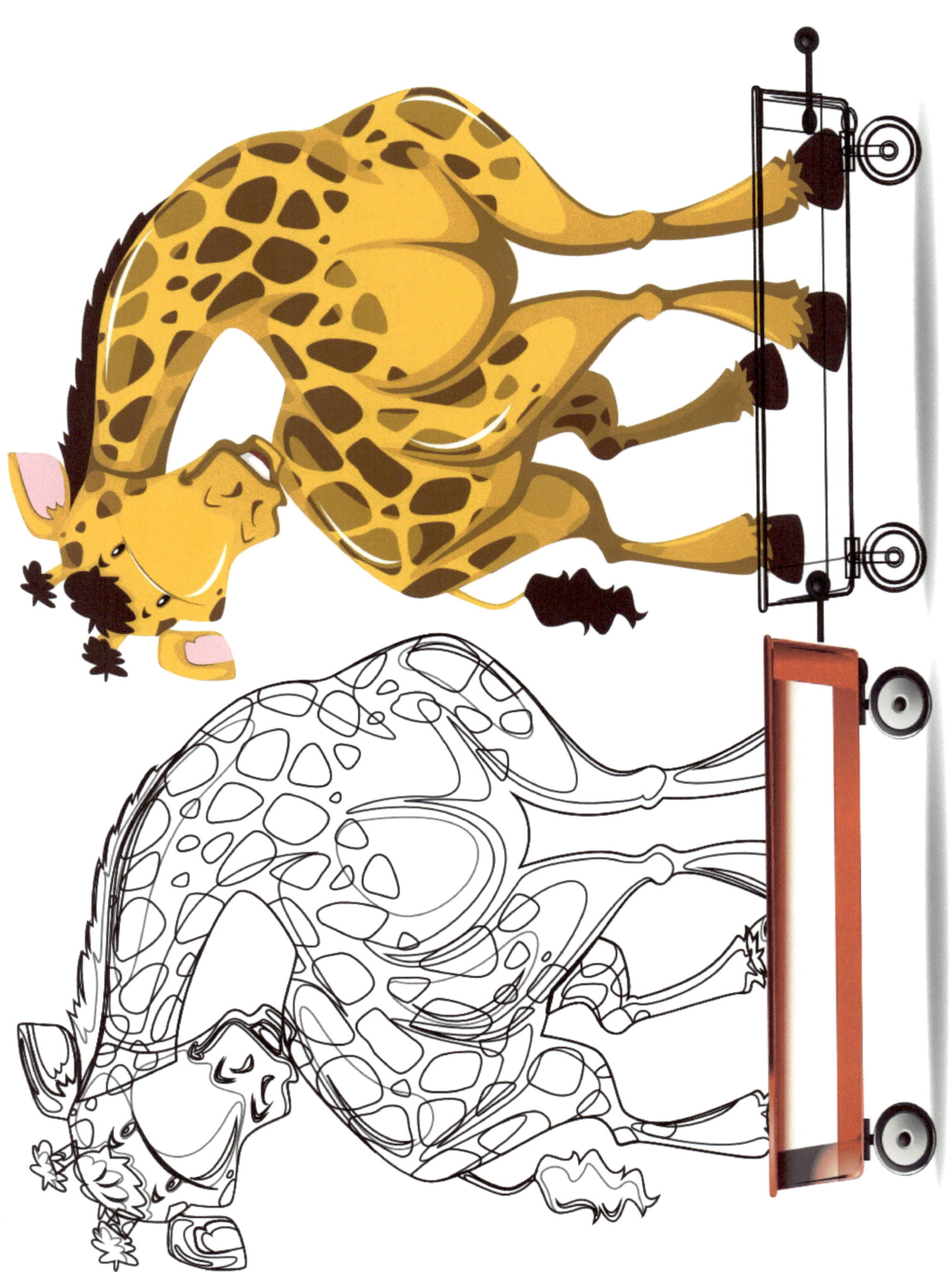

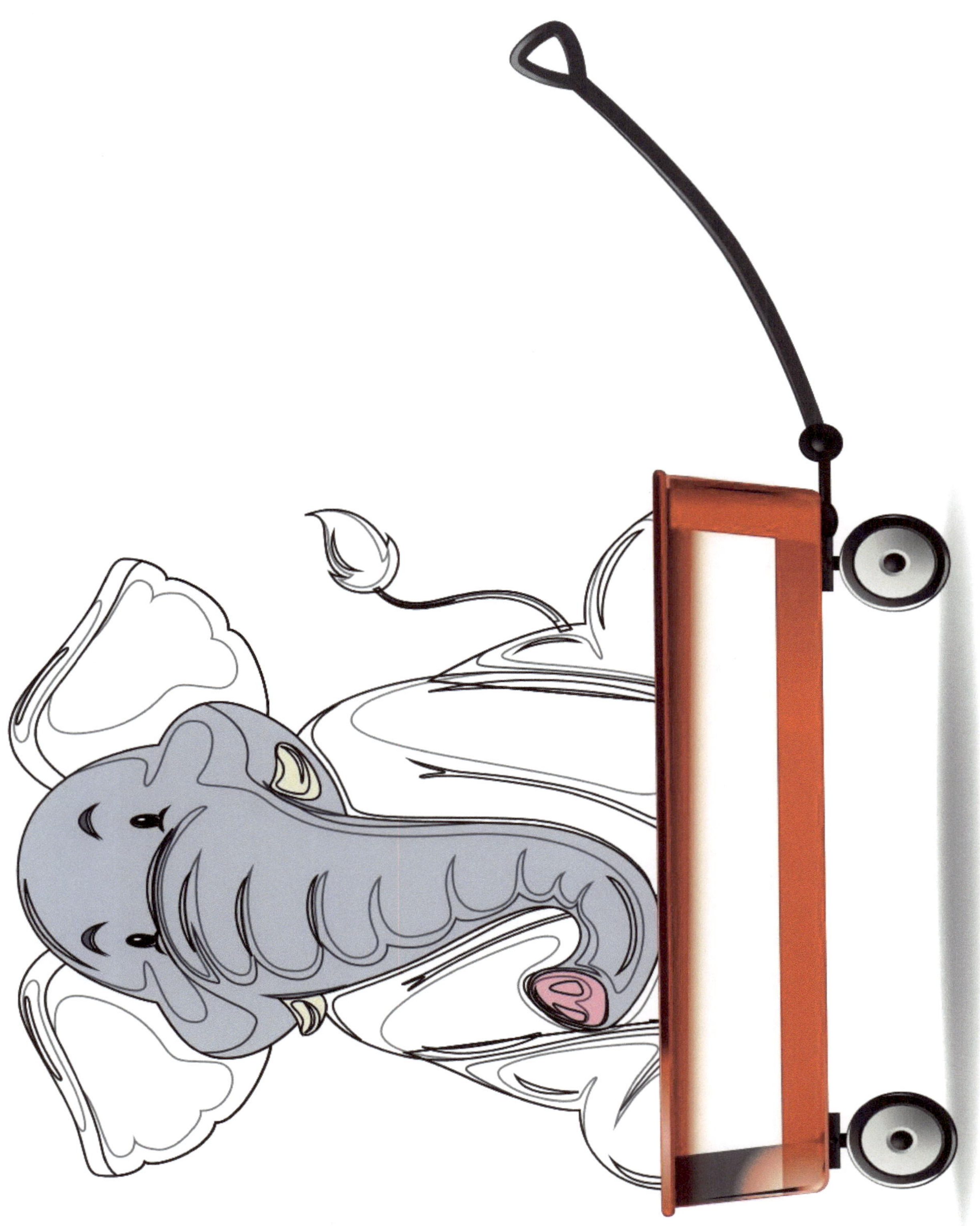

Draw you are a hero

Draw you are a hero

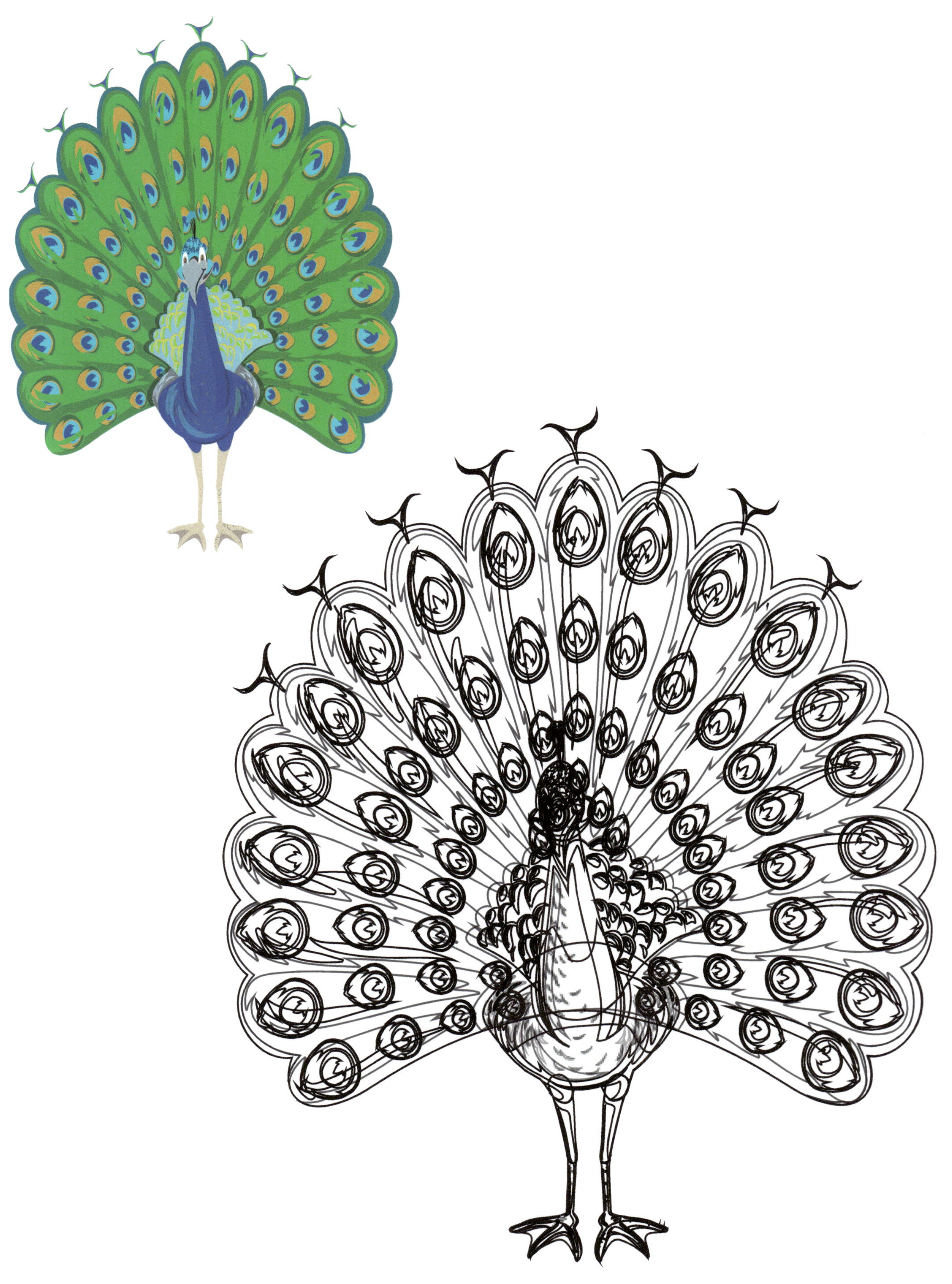